The Top 1%

The Mindsets Top Loan Officers Use that Take Them from Good to Great!

Ben Chenault

The Top 1%

Created with:
90-Minute Books
302 Martinique Drive
Winter Haven, FL 33884
www.90minutebooks.com

Copyright © 2019, Ben Chenault

Published in the United States of America

180108-00989-5

ISBN: 9781794573482
Imprint: Independently published

No parts of this publication may be reproduced without correct attribution to the author of this book.
For more information on 90-Minute Books including finding out how you can publish your own book, visit 90minutebooks.com or call (863) 318-0464

Here's What's Inside…

Introduction 1

It's the Little Bitty Things that Differentiate the Good from the Great 6

The 8 Mindsets of the Top 1%-ers 9

Mindset #1:
The Power of Personal Growth
and Ambition 13

Mindset #2:
CEO Mindset 17

Mindset #3:
Sense of Urgency 20

Mindset #4:
Your Team 25

Mindset #5:
Systematic and Proactive 28

Mindset #6:
Production Results 33

Mindset #7:
Competitive Mindset 35

Mindset #8:
Industry Lifestyle 39

Nicole's Story:
The Mindsets at Work Together...................... 43

Josh's Story:
An Interview with a Top Producer 54

Conclusion?... 79

Your Top Loan Officer Potential
Scorecard.. 83

Preface

"After 40 years leading some mortgage companies and production, as well as coaching successful leaders, I have been able to observe and watch many successful mortgage originators.

I'm delighted that Ben Chenault has provided a roadmap that can help originators live more productive and successful lives. Attitude and mindset is the foundation for success and you will get a lot out of this book and help more clients realize the American Dream."

Jerry Baker
Coach and Industry Legend

Introduction

The Top 1% of Loan Originators in the Nation.. How do they do it?

As a producing manager and team leader I have always wished there was a predictive tool to determine who would be a successful Loan Originator and who would not.

I've seen it all from sales assessments to personality profiles. Most were inconclusive in my opinion. My original intent in gathering all this information was to create a "scorecard" for myself that could help measure someone's potential.

After examining all the research, I decided it would be more effective to put my findings into a book to explain the "why" behind each section. There is so much more going on in the minds of Top Producers than a simple scorecard can capture. I'm not a writer or publisher. I'm a Loan Originator, which means I probably have ADD and an allergic condition to anything with details so please excuse my lack of writing skills. But don't worry, I had my processors and underwriters proof read everything before I sent it to the publisher. So I blame them for any grammatical errors because that's just what us LO's do! And I assume most LOs reading this book have the same attention span as I do, so I kept the chapters extra short for us!

Here it is….

I find it extremely interesting you can take two people who have the same set of tools available to them, and one person excels at what they do while the other person doesn't. They may work for the same company, have the same educational background, the same tools and apparent skillsets; yet, one makes it to the top 1% in the country, and the other one is mediocre at best.

We know if we took the average Joe/Jane and gave them the same geographical farming area, they wouldn't have nearly the success the top producer would have with the same exact resources at their disposal.

Have you ever stopped to wonder why that is? Or, why someone that was mediocre for years made a change and tripled (or more) their business inside of 12 months? I have.

Most of the time we just pass this observation off with the quick answer, "He or she is just a very driven person." That seems like a fair answer.

But what does that really mean? For me, it's too generic and doesn't tell what's really going on in someone's head. There seems to be an internal change or shift the top 1% has made which the rest of the population hasn't. What is it? Are they just super smart? What skills do they possess that others don't? What secret do they know that others don't? Is there a silver bullet? Is it their connections? Is it special school they went to?

Being a student of the industry, I have had a burning desire to answer the question, "Why is this top performer better than the others when they have all the same skill sets?"

In this book, I set out to identify what the distinction is between those at the top and the rest, so we can all learn and get better at what we do.

We were hoping to find a simple answer; maybe they're better connected or had a different upbringing. That would help them know more people and rise to the top. Or, maybe they had a better geographical farming area because they came from a different town. Or, maybe it was because they were involved in some networking groups which gave them a competitive advantage? We were hoping to find something the top 1% was doing differently, but the reality was they had different Mindsets than the average Joe.

They just think differently.

We wanted to figure out what those Mindsets were and how "the top" think differently. We then went out and interviewed many of those at the top to find out what makes them tick. We talked to industry experts, coaches, and veteran CEOs to get their opinions and insight.

We went back and forth with their answers until we narrowed them down to a few observations.

The short answer: It's **HOW** they think and what they **FOCUS** on that is the main differentiator. We discovered 8 Mindsets they have that the "average Joe" either doesn't have or doesn't act upon in their business life. These Mindsets and their descriptions are discussed in this short book.

It's important to note there are a lot of other factors which go into being a successful loan officer that everyone possesses.

Every loan officer needs to have certain things to be in the game. You have to have a client. You have to care about your client. You must have the technical knowledge and understand guidelines. You have to be able to connect with people. You have to be a good communicator. You can't just be about the dollar. That's the price of admission to do a good and decent job.

After the basics, these 8 Mindsets are the things the 1% have and portray which most people don't. These 8 Mindsets are what the top 1% use to take it to a different level.

After you understand the logic behind these 8 Mindsets discussed in these short chapters, you can take your own assessment at www.lopotential.com. I suggest taking the assessment every quarter to you can track you progress and see where your focus needs be directed for that quarter.

I hope this book gives you insights into what separates those at the top and how they think differently. And I hope this book inspires some to change their Mindsets to become a top producer if they wish to be!

To Your Success!

Ben

It's the Little Bitty Things that Differentiate the Good from the Great

Many loan officers are happy where they are in their career and many are even content. But many more, are frustrated with the results they are getting.

The average loan officer in America does between 2 and 3 loans per month. People can make a living on that with minimal effort. Good loan officers do 8 to 10 loans a month. They put forth tons of effort, and see results, but they are missing a couple of key ingredients to get them to the next level.

There's a Zig Ziglar quote that says something to the effect of, "What's the difference between a $1 million-dollar racehorse and a $5 million racehorse? Is the $5 million racehorse five times as fast?" No. The $5 million horse is a *nose faster*.

That's it, a little bit faster and yet it's everything. I recall watching the Olympics; I was constantly amazed at the time difference between first place and tenth place in things like the Men's downhill or luge. We are talking about hundredths of a second which separate the best in the world from a non-mentionable.

That's it, but those hundredths of a second are what matter the most.

It's the same in our industry. It's these little bitty things multiplied or compounded over time which make the difference between a top producer and somebody who's just good at their job.

If you ask good loan officers who are doing between 8 and 10 loans a month, they may tell you they're frustrated or on the verge of burnout. They're tired of working long hours, doing the same thing, month in and month out, without things getting dramatically better.

What's missing for them are the Mindsets the Top 1% have which allow them to work hard but have levels of success that are 10 or 100 times greater than an average loan officer.

If you're not currently a top performer, it's not too late! There have been many top LOs that were average producers for years - Until one day, something changed. They made a decision to change how they thought, focused, and implemented.

No matter where you are in your career, you too can make that same shift using the same 8 Mindsets the top loan officers in the nation use.

The 8 Mindsets of the Top 1%-ers

How did we come up with these specific 8 Mindsets? By asking questions and then asking them again we isolated these Mindsets.

I've been involved in several industry events. I know a lot of mortgage people because I live it and breathe it every day, so I have access to some of the top people in the industry. Many are friends. We've traveled together, we've visited one another's offices, and our spouses know each other. For these producer's, we simply asked, "What do you think it takes to make it to the top?"

Some rattled off their answers in 20 seconds. Others pondered the question for days. For some, success and achievement came so naturally they had a hard time noticing what they did. It was like asking LeBron James how to be a great basketball player.

Also, knowing people can't always see in themselves what others see, we spoke to those around them. We asked their coaches and co-workers. We also spoke to industry experts for their opinions and insight into "HOW" the top performers thought. For this group we asked, "What do you think makes a good loan officer great?"

I wrote down what they told me and started overlaying my observations. I tried to pay attention to things which most people don't pay attention to. I looked for the "answers behind the answers." There were certain common themes that appeared.

It's not how somebody is doing it, but *how did they think through getting to this point.* **HOW** they think separates them from the rest. When we build the spectrums of Mindset in the next chapters, these are Mindsets everyone has. But you have different degrees in which you live them.

For example, most people have some competitive nature in them, but the degree of competitiveness changes from individual to individual, thus the degree of intensity in each Mindset. Top performers tend to have a high degree of intensity in each one of these Mindsets. All the Mindsets work in tandem. That's another thing I found interesting. You can have a higher degree of intensity (thus higher score) in some areas and less in others. It's almost like if you added up all the scores, you're still going to have a high overall score. But if you want to grow your business, you have to pay attention to them all and how they relate to one another.

Each of the Mindsets has a potential score from 1-12. We need to rate ourselves (truthfully) where we are today but more importantly, where we want to be in the future.

Note: The gap between the present and future is the most important factor! That will tell you what you need to work on or develop a passion around.

Shocking Discovery: I found it very interesting NONE of the top LOs rated themselves a 12 on ANYTHING! They ALL thought they could improve in every area and felt like tomorrow will be better than today! None of them felt like they were perfect, without flaw, or could not improve upon where they were now. They all had an optimistic view of their future potential growth even though they had already achieved a very high level of success in their field.

Picture each of the Mindsets as a spoke on a wheel. If one spoke was insufficient, the wheel would not roll smoothly. The same can be said for any major area in one's business. An insufficient (Mindset) area would also create an issue in one's production. They all matter.

Mindset #1: The Power of Personal Growth and Ambition

I know a great loan officer we will call him "Paul." During the 1998-2006 timeframe, Paul was "the man" in his area. He had more market share than any other LO in his medium- sized market. All the realtors knew him and referred only to him. All the other loan officers hated to compete against him because he had a great mix of salesmanship and technical ability.

Paul consistently closed between $50 mill and $60 mill a year with an average loan amount less than $200k which were great numbers back then. He was on top of his game. Then one day he decided to go into management for a few years. When he returned to originating a few years later, he discovered things had changed a bit while he was away from originating. He thought he could re-enter the LO role and get back in the game. He did everything exactly the way he did previously. He took Realtors and Financial Advisors to lunch. He delivered doughnuts and dropped off product flyers. He attended Real Estate Caravans and took rate sheets to pass around. He was first to get into the office and last to leave. He stayed in his office on the phone all day and even processed his own loans. Paul refused to utilize technology, social media, or even new modes of communication. After all, he was a legend and didn't need any of that "stuff." He didn't need those things in the previous years, so why would he need it now, right?

Wrong.

We all know how it turned out for Paul. He worked extra hard, did honest work, but never rose above the "Average" threshold. In fact, he was mediocre at best. For those that worked around him, it was tough to watch such disappointment. Everyone knew his previous status and was expecting to see him on top again. It was like watching Rocky Balboa get beat up. The industry (and the client) changed but he refused to change with it.

Some people become students of themselves and their growth matches their ambition.

On the other hand you have the ones that read gossip magazines or play on social media in their free time. Some people are frightened by change.

They're trying to keep things the same so they can keep up.

On the other end of the spectrum, top producers are always looking for ways to grow and expand and change.

They're always trying to be a better version of themselves.

"The Great" loan officer takes extra steps to grow. They attend seminars, not only mortgage-related, but business-related or self-help. They listen to podcasts when they exercise or download audio books. Most have hired a business coach to help critique how they can become a better version of themselves and grow their business.

"The Good" loan officer understands all of those things are important. *But,* they'll grow when it's convenient (which it never is). They'll attend a seminar if it's convenient so they can check the attendance box. They don't do it with the same vigor as a top producer.

"Top Producers" tend to crave information. They need to get better. They seek out people who can help them. It's like a professional golfer who hires the best swing coach there is, to break down and analyze their swing so they can get a little more distance or consistency. Their swing was already good enough to make it on the Pro Tour, but they want to make it even better.

"The Average" loan officer is a self-doer: like Paul, they think they have it figured out, they don't want to spend the time, energy, or effort to check themselves. They don't hire a coach because they're afraid of what the coach might tell them. In general, they tend to be okay with status quo, personally and professionally. They may put the hours in but without the focus or passion. I call this being "Mentally Lazy."

All Top loan officers have a relentless thirst to improve themselves.

Where are you on the spectrum?

How willing are you to take your personal growth to the next level?

Mindset #2: CEO Mindset

Most loan originators look at their job as a job.

They don't look at it as a career. The average loan officer still expects their company to provide them all the tools and resources they need to do their job.

"The average" or "the good" loan officer looks at it as an employer/employee relationship. Like the old banking-type model. They clock in at 8:00 and leave at 5:00. They want to come in and check all the boxes at the end, then go home after collecting their *good-enough-for-today* paycheck.

Great loan officers and top 1%-ers, however, take what I call a "CEO Mindset." They look at their business as "Them Inc." or "You Inc." Even though they work for a bank or a mortgage lender, they still consider themselves a self-employed entity that has revenue and expenses. They don't count on anyone else to help their career other than themselves. They go out and explore the tools they need to make their business a success. They invest their own time and money into products like Mortgage Coach or their own CRM system because it enhances their client's experience. They look at these as an investment in their business. They also do their own research about guidelines or even new technology. They are aware of new products and trends and take the time to research and learn how they can help their business.

They don't wait for their company to provide the information or wait for their boss to come give them a 30-minute lesson. They don't count on their company to provide them leads. They don't depend on their company to provide the direction, either.

I recently attended a local MBA event and spoke to a long-time loan officer I have known for some time. We exchanged the usual pleasantries and I asked him how his business was going. His response floored me. He said, "It would be doing a lot better if they would hire me an assistant and give me a decent portfolio product."

Really?

I quickly realized why he was just an average producer even though he had been in the business for many years. He was totally relying on what his company would provide for him. He wasn't thinking like a CEO willing to grow his own team or develop better sales skills. Why is it someone else's responsibility to grow his team or provide a unique niche product for him to compete in the marketplace with everyone else?

Top Producers look at themselves as a self-employed machine and take total responsibility for their outcomes.

They make the mental shift between having a job versus having a career; then to the next step of having a business. The top 1% considers themselves a business owner, even though they work for someone else. They don't depend on their company for a marketing plan, lead generation, or anything else.

They sure don't count on the company to go out and pay for everything. If they have a need, they handle the need. If there are tools and products they need, they go out and purchase them. Then they invest the time to learn how to use them in their business. If they want to grow into a team, they may fund it themselves because they understand the payoffs could be big.

They understand their success or failure is totally their responsibility.

Mindset #3: Sense of Urgency

Sense of urgency is how quickly someone will make decisions and how quickly they're asking the questions, "What's next? Who's next? How fast can we get it done?"

For the discussion in Mindset 3, we are referring to urgency in all areas of a loan officer's business life. It's measured by how fast they call someone back, how fast they handle a loan file, and most importantly how fast they implement new ideas.

In life, many people are afraid of doing things others perceive as pushy. They let life happen at its own pace or whenever things come to them. It's like being in a boat going down a river. Wherever the river takes them is where they're going to end up, and they feel like they don't have a whole lot of control over it, nor do they want to change it. They think the industry may change, and when it does, they'll make their adjustments. They think when a client is ready to move forward, the client will call them back. They also think everything happens in time, and when the time is right, things will present themselves.

The top 1%-ers chase the change and opportunities. They have a sense of urgency about everything. They believe things need to happen now before something else changes. It's almost as if they have a fear that, if they don't grab it now, it'll be gone, whatever it is.

They have a sense of urgency which means, "I have to get something done today instead of tomorrow because tomorrow will bring its own set of problems." "I will not go home with emails not answered or voicemails not returned." "I must call people back quickly or I may lose the deal!" "I must investigate the new tools quickly." "I must hire new teammates quickly." "I have to move at a pace so that no one else can catch up to me." Even if they only have 2 minutes before an appointment and they receive a client message, they call that client back immediately to schedule a better time to talk.

They know that client could call another lender within minutes.

Average producers can be very ho-hum about everything they do from prospecting, developing relationships, making outbound phone calls, handling loan fires, making adjustments with the team, and everything else involving their business.

The top 1%-ers seem to move at a pace ten times the speed of the average producer, yet they're no smarter. They work no harder. They're more focused and proactive in everything they do, including their follow-up with anyone who can help them grow their business. And did I mention….they implement new ideas…. FAST.

Many years ago I attended an Industry Event in Las Vegas. It was sales focused and put on by one of the long-time legends in the Industry. There were many top producers on stage from all over the Country. They were explaining their best secrets that helped them bring more business in the door and stay on top of their game.

The auditorium was packed and everyone was taking notes like they were hearing the secrets to the universe. One of the high-producing speakers on stage mentioned his hometown was Las Vegas and made a joke that he didn't have to travel too far to attend this event.

I found this very interesting because I assumed that many of his local competitors were in the audience. After all, they didn't have to travel far either. And why wouldn't they want to hear what this guy was doing in their shared market?

This really bothered me for some reason. I wasn't sure if I could ever share my business plans with the competition. How was he able to share so freely with them? I needed to know what he was thinking. So I waited until the break and did what any sane person would do - I stalked him down to get some answers.

I asked him "Does it bother you so many of your competitors are in the audience and hearing what you are doing to steal their market share?" His response forever changed how I look at Urgency and Implementation.

He turned to me and said "Nope. Less than 5% of those in the audience will ever implement 1 idea they heard at this event. Most of them are fully satisfied with gaining the knowledge but will never doing anything about it. They will feel like they got their money's worth and go back to the office tomorrow, play catch up from attending this event, and probably never review the notes they took.

Even if they did implement something, I'm so far ahead with tomorrow's projects, they would never catch up anyway."

Having a new idea and never doing anything about it would be like joining a new gym so you can live a healthier lifestyle. You go through all the membership classes, you learn how to use the new machines, and you pay the monthly membership fees. Congratulations! You are now part of the exercise community. Feels great, right?

Nope. We all know you will never be any healthier until you do something! Simply joining and gaining the knowledge will not help make you healthier. Yet millions do it every year; same as in this business. No one can do your pushups for you!

You have to implement and do it with a strong sense of urgency or nothing will ever change.

Mindset #4: Your Team

The average loan officer is a team of one: themselves.

Most can max out at about 8 to 10 loans a month if they work hard. The average loan officer is scared to hire a team member because they're too concerned about, "What if things slow down? I don't want the overhead."

For them, hiring somebody is an expense, not an investment in themselves.

They may recognize the job of an LO is laden with "non-revenue generating" activities. There's a lot of paperwork, but they don't want to expend the time, energy, or money to bring in someone to help them do it or spend the brain power to identify how that would even look.

Besides that, they would have to train them and who has time for that? Top 1%-ers, on the other hand, understand the concept of team, and they understand what their unique ability is.

They try to delegate every activity other than their unique ability. They understand they only get paid to structure loans and create relationships, period.

Nothing else.

These Top Producers do a great job at delegating all the other functions a loan officer is faced with. On their team, each position is strategically broken down and everyone knows their roll on that team. Let's be clear – we have all seen teams fail. There are plenty of people that have gone out and recklessly hired warm bodies, took on excessive overhead, and lost money because they failed to strategize and pay attention to the numbers (see Mindset #2). Top 1% Producer views a well-run team like a company inside of a company.

Top producing teams are all dialed in, and the business model itself becomes something larger than that of the top 1%-er loan officer. It's an entity which moves on its own whether that loan officer is in the office or not. It works because they have team members who are dialed in and have everything rolling.

Top 1%-ers can have teams of 2 or 30. Regardless of their size, they are always continuing to grow their business. As they grow, their vision allows them to create new positions that keep a predictable model sustained. They cover everything from lead generation to deal structuring and coordinating closings. They have people who specialize in every part of the loan process. They don't worry about the added expense bringing more people on will create but rather get excited about the opportunities that more people will bring into the company.

Again, I'm not proposing carelessly hiring people to do your job. Top Producers have a business plan and pro-forma of revenue and expenses before they ever start the interview process.

They never start without a careful plan in place first.

Mindset #5: Systematic and Proactive

The average loan officer comes in each morning without a plan.

Most show up between 8:30 and 9:30. They boot up their laptop, see if they've gotten any emails. They'll respond to a few emails; then they'll get up and get some coffee. They'll talk to their processor and ask about a couple of loans. Then they go back to their desk, and by that time, they've received a few more emails to respond to, so they'll spend some time doing that.

They may make a follow-up call or two, and before they know it, it's lunchtime. They leave with their coworker and go to lunch for 60 to 90 minutes. They come back and do the same thing in the afternoon they did in the morning. They do this year after year after year. Many feel like, as long as they put their 40 hours of work in, they should receive a good paycheck at the end of the year. And the truth is, most do, but they're average at best.

Now contrast this against some of the top 1%-ers who start their days at 4:00 or 5:00 in the morning so they can get it all in.

Their day is usually planned out many, many days before. They know exactly what they're going to be doing and when they will be doing it, sometimes weeks ahead of time, but at a minimum, the night before. When they show up in the office the next day, they already have a plan of action they work from the moment they walk through the door.

There is zero downtime, zero social media time unless they're using it for prospecting. Everything is systematic and proactive for these people. They are focused only on business-generating activities, regardless of what's happening around them. Many of the top 1%-ers complete their entire prospecting efforts before they even look at their email in the morning. Think about that for a moment.

Having everything mapped out and having systems for everything affords them the ability to handle 10x the workload than an average loan officer.

A system is defined as a predetermined action or predetermined reaction to any action that comes in. It's a routine that is followed on every loan, every time.

They have a system for any new client phone calls, any Realtor questions or loan processing milestones. They have mastered the "if this, then that" in everything. This has enabled them to delegate it to their team so they can remain proactive in what is making them successful.

The top 1%-ers are extremely systematic and proactive about their time.

That's why I put this Mindset right after the team Mindset. They go hand in hand. Knowing we all have the same number of hours in a day, their team allows them to stay focused on generating business.

A story that comes to mind is the one every business school student has heard.

A teacher walks into a classroom and sets a glass jar on the table. He silently places 2-inch rocks in the jar until no more can fit. He asks the class if the jar is full and they agree it is. He says, "Really," and pulls out a pile of small pebbles, adding them to the jar, shaking it slightly until they fill the spaces between the rocks.

He asks again, "Is the jar full?" They agree. So next, he adds a scoop of sand to the jar, filling the space between the pebbles and asks the question again. This time, the class is divided, some feeling that the jar is obviously full, but others are wary of another trick. He grabs a pitcher of water and fills the jar to the brim, saying, "If this jar is your life, what does this experiment show you?"

A bold student replies, "No matter how busy you think you are, you can always take on more." "That is one view," he replies. Then he looks out at the class making eye contact with everyone, "The rocks represent the BIG things in your life – what you will value at the end of your life – your family, your partner, your health, fulfilling your hopes and dreams.

The pebbles are the other things in your life that give it meaning, like your job, your house, your hobbies, your friendships.

The sand and water represent the 'small stuff' that fills our time, like watching TV or running errands." Looking out at the class again, he asks, "Can you see what would happen if I started with the sand or the pebbles?"

Although this story represents life and the things a person deems important to them, it can easily be applied to how one handles their business. For a top producer, their "big rocks" are always PROACTIVE PROSPECTING!

Calling on referral sources or prospective clients take precedence over everything.

Several of those interviewed have even adopted a daily "power hour (or two)" where they shut down email, have a team member respond to their incoming calls, and shut themselves off to everything else happening around them so they can focus only on making outbound calls to those prospects. They know their day will be a success as long as these calls are made.

We all know there are many other things a loan officer is responsible for like pipeline management, underwriting surprises, inspection issues to name a few, but those are all handled outside prospecting times.

Top producers know they are important but each of those activities represent the pebbles, sand, and water in the story above.

One coach commented he believes the average loan officer spends about 4 hours each week prospecting but claim they work at least 40 hours a week. So, what are they doing with those remaining 36 hours?

Are you really prospecting enough to reach your potential?

Mindset #6: Production Results

Although Production Results is more of a measurable activity than a Mindset, we had to put it in because it was mentioned by everyone we interviewed.

After all, everything discussed in this book is measured by top loan officers and expected to achieve one thing: RESULTS! For them, positive results create a bigger high than the pain it took to achieve them.

Top Producing LOs measure everything. They measure leads coming in per source, conversion, follow up calls made, inbound calls, and current client referrals, for instance. They test new scripts, marketing, email templates, and everything else that is a part of their business model. They think in terms of ROI or LOI (Loans on Investment). They ask questions like, "by adding this marketing plan or entering this new business relationship how many more loans will we produce? Will the commissions generated by those new loans pay for costs to obtain them?" Or, "If I added another dialer to call all leads older than 120 days, could I increase my closings by an average of 5 per month?"

The average loan officer will do one to three loans a month, which is quite sad when you look at it. They're not getting out there and getting a lot of business done. Good loan officers can hit seven or maybe even 8 loans a month. Maybe they can hit 10 to 12 in spike months or hot buying months. The top 1%, however, are usually going to average well over 15 loans per month.

In fact, many of the folks I've talked to do well over 50 loans a month.

What needs to be different to allow one loan officer to close 8 loans a month while another one closes 50 loans?

This Mindset is the accumulation of all the other Mindsets. The other 7 Mindsets are what allow the 1%-ers to close the number of loans they do month after month after month.

Mindset #7: Competitive Mindset

Out of all the Mindsets explored, this is the one every person I spoke to mentioned. I'm not saying it's the most important, I am saying every person I asked brought up being competitive as something the 1%-ers do better than anyone else.

The average loan officer doesn't seem to have the same passion or drive to be very competitive. Maybe they once did. Maybe having a family has slowed them down. It doesn't matter. But, today, they don't have the Mindset to be competitive in this business.

Some may even be competitive in other areas of their life. There are plenty of average loan officers out there who are super-competitive in sports. Many may be athletes in some shape, form, or fashion, but they haven't found a way to translate that into their business (see Nicole's story towards end of book). The top 1%-ers have figured out how to transfer their competitiveness to their business.

When we talk about being competitive, it's not the fact that you're a competitive person in general. It's the fact you're a competitive person in this industry. Being competitive with a sibling playing cards doesn't matter in the mortgage business.

But, for the top 1%-ers, they took that competitive streak and figured out how it applied to their business. Not only do they compete with the people in their office (in a friendly way), but they also compete against themselves to be better and better. They compete with every competitor, and they want to win.

Top Producers are so competitive that it seems to transcend everything else. This goes against what most people would think is a biggest motivator or driver: money. It's the competitiveness to win, that's a huge breakthrough.

I'm not suggesting money doesn't matter to them. They seem to care so much more about winning and the money is just the byproduct or a measuring stick. They adopt the famous words of Ricky Bobby: "If you ain't first, you're last!"

They understand there are no participation awards. This is real life, and they want to topple their competition. The fact that money wasn't the biggest motivator for almost all we interviewed was a huge surprise. Some of the people we looked at worked for the same company, and when the monthly production reports come out, they open them immediately trying to find out where they're ranked.

These people are highly competitive in their field. The competitiveness is what drives them to excel in these other Mindsets. It makes them willing to do whatever it takes to be the best in their business.

Maybe you've lost the drive you once had, or maybe you never had it to begin with, but every loan officer must realize they are competing every day whether they want to or not. This is a competition that can be life or death. The winner of this competition is you, your family, and all of your hopes and dreams.

I've seen people who were uber-competitive. They will fist-fight you over a corn hole tournament, but they don't care to go out and make sales calls. The fact is they do have the tools. They have the skill; they just haven't figured out yet how to use their competitive spirit to create the desire. If you know you are competing anyway, why not win?

Another observation of the Top LOs is how they feel about their teams sharing in the "wins." Since most of them have a team (small or large), they seem to have developed a higher degree of competitiveness because they are also rooting for their team's success. Knowing they have other families counting on them and the successes and the failures are part of that, they get a "This is bigger than just me; we have to win, Coach" mentality.

Mindset #8: Industry Lifestyle

This Mindset was a surprising discovery.

I've noticed it before, but it wasn't until I interviewed many other loan officers that it became blatantly obvious.

The Top 1% Producers really enjoys this business. "Average" loan originators look at going to an industry event or seminar as a total pain in the rear end. They don't want to take away from their three to five loans a month. They don't want to invest the money nor the time to attend. They won't take the time away. It is a thorn in their side, and they have zero enjoyment out of it, whereas the top 1%-ers try to attend as many of these events as possible.

They don't go because they're workaholics. It's because they want to go and they have fun, too. Yes I said it – Fun!

Average loan officers consider this a job.

When they go home on Friday, their mind is elsewhere. As soon as they clock out, they're done. They feel like business hours are business hours, and my personal hours are my personal hours, and they do not coexist. Top 1%-ers, however, feel like their time continuum is all one.

They mix and mingle throughout personal and business because it's all the same. They don't always take it to an unhealthy level. The reasoning for this is because it's not just work, it's also their hobby. Sitting around talking shop, visiting with other top loan originators, and getting ideas is fun. It's not a chore. Let's face it, none of us grew up wanting to be a Loan Officer. It just isn't as cool as a Fireman, Police Officer, or Doctor. So, being passionate and loving this business is a CHOICE. Top 1%-ers chose to develop a passion for this business.

The average loan officer may read sports magazines or gossip column magazines in their spare time. Many of the top 1% enjoys reading industry publications or blog's like Rob Chrisman's daily commentary because they enjoy getting better at what they do. Being a good loan officer isn't just what they do, it's who they are.

Every business book, every TED Talk idea, they filter through the lens of mortgage originating (see Josh Mettle's interview). They take all the great ideas, and try to figure out, "How can that work in my business?"

I'm not saying the Top 1%-ers just work 24/7 and don't have a life! In fact, most seem to have a great work/life balance. Many of the top 1% may be working some over the weekend, but they still attend their kid's recital on Tuesday afternoon and have date nights with their spouses. They may always be "on" to some extent even if it's through their team helping them get it all done.

When I attend some of the industry events around the country, what I find very interesting are the "meetings after the meeting."

You can always find a group of top performers sitting in a corner, sharing a drink and sharing ideas. They can sit there for hours laughing, cutting up, telling stories, and also learning and sharing. Because loan origination is what they do, they don't see talking about it as a chore. They enjoy it so much that many people in our industry have gained strong friendships with others even though they work for different companies in different parts of the country.

Being a top producing mortgage originator is a current bond they have. Many of these people hang out together, travel together, talk on a monthly basis together, and form mastermind groups. They're not just associates, they're friends, too. They all speak the same language.

The next time you attend an event like Todd Duncan's Sales Mastery, pay attention to the guys and gals speaking on stage. Not only do they all know one another, most of them are friends. But you may have already recognized that.

Nicole's Story: The Mindsets at Work Together

Let me share with you one particular story about a loan officer who was pretty average for years.

Nicole Rueth had a pretty dynamic background when it came to closing loans, but she didn't stand out. This is her story of how she went from someone on the verge of burnout to becoming a Top Producer. She made some adjustments and something happened. She flipped the switch, and it changed her Mindsets. She became very competitive in this business. She went from a $24 Mill to $100 Mill/year producer in only 4 years.

Nicole was a successful athlete. She was very competitive when it came to working out in the gym and competing. She was extremely healthy when it came to her eating. She was extremely disciplined in everything she did, but she didn't care much about being a top loan officer. Her zeal in life was outside of work.

She had no passion for being a Loan Originator.

She became a natural food chef and a health coach on the side as she tried to remove herself from, as she put it, "all the bullshit that was happening".

Here's her story:

> *All the compliance and regulations were frustrating me, and I felt like I was beating my head up against the wall trying to navigate through it all. I was ready to quit when a friend of mine wooed me and suggested we do it as a team. It sounded like the right answer at the time, but it turned out to be a complete disaster.*
>
> *I was thinking about getting out of the business when another friend reached out. We looked at doing corporate training because I was done with the whole originating thing. I'd done it for a couple of years and was burned out. I was doing maybe four to five loans a month at the time, and it didn't seem like it was worth all the hassle.*
>
> *I hired my first coach (Mindset #1), and he would always start our conversation with, 'So, where are we at today? Are we all in?' My answer as always, 'Well, no, not yet. I'm*

checking out this thing over here, and I'm checking out this thing over here. Do I want to be in commercial lending? Do I want to get out of the business and do corporate training?'

The truth is I wasn't 'all-in.' I was always eyeing something greener. I didn't want to commit all in, as I had no passion for the business. He kept persisting and kept asking me if I was all in yet.

Then he switched gears. He finally said to me, 'At some point, you're going to get tired of not knowing what you want to do.' He was spot on because I was doing this, I was doing that, and then I was doing something else. At some point, it resonated deep within me. I was getting so tired of figuring out what I wanted to be when I grew up. And I was like, 'I have to grow up. This is it. I either have to be here, or I have to get out.'

From there, I committed myself, and to my coach at the time, 'Okay. I'm all in. Let's get all in. Let's put the people on the bus and see what happens.'

It's amazing what a difference that made. All of a sudden, I started getting excited about the opportunity in front of me. I started to have the goals. Okay, I want to get to Chairman's Club ($45 mill). At that time, Platinum Club (Top LO) didn't even *exist, but I set these goals that were always outside of what I thought I could do.*

What was the difference? I'm a competitor by nature. I'm born to be. But, at the time, I wasn't a competitor in this part of my world. I was doing figure competing. I was doing adventure racing. I was doing bike rides. I was doing triathlons. I was expressing my competitiveness in my sports life. I couldn't figure out what this looked like in my career life. And then when I finally decided to be all in with my work, that's when the competitive mind shift switched (Mindset #7). Like it wasn't a day job to pay my bills anymore, now it was like I wanted to see how far I could go.

I'm never, never competitive to the lane next to me. I'm self-competitive. I need to be better than I was last time. I tell myself what ranking I want, or what top percentage I want. And I need to be in there, and if I'm not there yet, I'm going to be (Mindset #1). But I don't care what the guy next to me is doing.

The guy next to me could have done twice as fast as me, and if I hit my number, it was a win in my book. It's important to set that goal, or you have nothing to shoot for. You just show up and get some work done. If you have a goal to hit, then everything is more on point, everything has a purpose, and everything is important and needs to get done today not tomorrow (Mindset #3).

I started doing vision boarding at this time. This was huge for me because I am so visual. Putting my goals up visually was a huge inspiration. To see it every single day motivates you as nothing else can.

My vision board back then was a collage of the car I wanted, which I got last year. Now for this year, I have the car I want to buy my husband. So, it was the car. It was the number of loans I want to hit (Mindset #6). Last time it was $80 mill, and I missed it by two. I got $78 mill. This time, it was $100 mill, and we went one over. So, that's big.

I include, 'How many families do we need to impact to do that?' I also add a picture of my team, who are making this happen with me (Mindset #4). And I include personal goals, too. I want a date night every week. I want a night with the kids every month. I have all those goals. And I have athletic goals on there, too, because that's still part of who I am.

Everything switched for me when I could design the vision of what I wanted my business to be. When I wasn't all in, I had no purpose in being there. I was coming to work and doing my job and making my calls. Somebody would tell me I had to make five calls a day or ten calls a day; I got that. And I can do that even without heart. I can get in there and do my job without vision, without passion, but now, all of a sudden, when I decided, 'Okay, I'm all in,' it became so much bigger.

It wasn't all smooth sailing. I had some hiccups, and I started a do-over. In fact, I had a lot of do-overs. At first, I thought I would bring in a bunch of other loan officers. I was interviewing people, but then I decided, 'No, it's going to center on me, and I'm going to build the team that supports that' (Mindset #2).

Then it was a process of deciding, 'What does that look like?' Somewhere along the line, my coach had me writing out the story. On December 31st, what does that look like? What does that team look like? What's the volume you hit? What's the process? What's the perfect loan process? He made me write all that out. I didn't want to write that out. I don't write documents. I go by the seat of my pants.

But I decided to trust him, and so I stopped and wrote out the vision, and I wrote out the story. I wrote out the perfect loan process (Mindset #5). Then, all of a sudden, it became crystal clear what it was I was building. Then it was easy from there. Everything is laid out, so you are back to checking off boxes. Then you're like, 'I can make my ten calls a day. But now I have a different, bigger purpose than the calls.

It's about deciding what you want. And that's something I'm constantly on my coaching my team about. They have to decide what they want. They can decide they want this, or they can decide they want that. I don't care what it is. But, they're going to get whatever that is they decide they want. So, you have to decide what you want, and then you have to design what that looks like.

Another element would be to own the process:

'This is mine. I'm going to design it how I want it' (Mindset #2). And in every environment you can get quickly sucked into other stuff, like the corporate stuff, the political stuff, the social stuff. It doesn't matter what company it is. You slap a different name on it; it's the same stuff. But, you have to decide what you want because we have this huge opportunity that we can design whatever we want. We get to set the course.

This is a good and a bad thing. That pissed me off at first because I'm a structure girl and I like the corporate structure. I liked somebody telling me, 'Here's the plan from A to Z.' It took a while to figure out what that plan was and what I wanted it to be (Mindset #2).

I think the switch flipped when I decided to be all in and then went through the process of designing what that looked like, and then laying the foundation for it and then in deciding who's the roles were (Mindset#4).

There are still people who come up to me and talk to me about, 'Well, who do I need on my team, and what do they do, and what roles should they have?' Nobody told me that. I had to figure that out through trial and error and to be honest, through a lot of mistakes. But, then knowing now part of that vision I have written out says, 'And David is on my team, and this is his title, and this is what he does. Then there's somebody I'm going to hire, this is their role, this is what they do, and this is how everybody reports to each other and supports each other (Mindset #4).

At first, I hired people and tried to figure out how to make them work. I had a loan officer assistant and a processor. And I was like, 'I don't have enough hours in the day.' So, I hired a personal assistant, and I felt guilty about it. I was like, 'What do I do with a personal assistant? Do I make them get my dry cleaning? Do they answer my emails?' I didn't know what to do with her.

So, I hired this girl, who's still with me two and a half, three years later. I hired her from California, and I said, 'I don't know what I'm going to have you do yet, but I'm going to pay you for forty hours. Come to work.

It sounds so lazy to have them go get my lunch. But it comes down to what a half-hour of your time is worth. I don't make her wash my car, but she does order my lunch.

The other thing is I think you have to be willing to take risks. You have to be willing to have the year I had to put the numbers on the board I did. If you're not willing to hire some people who make you uncomfortable or that do and try things that make you uncomfortable, you'll never get there. You have to be willing to fall on your face.

Then you have to be willing to put the work in. Nobody's going to make this easier. You can't hire more people to work less. It doesn't work that way. You have to lead by example, and you have to be there. You can get to a point when you can take Fridays off but if you don't set the stage; your people will never over perform either. They will mimic you. So, if I don't show them I'm willing to answer a phone call at 8:30 or 9 o'clock at night, they'll never answer a phone call at 8:30 or 9 o'clock at night.

I've worked my ass off this year. I sacrificed other stuff. You have to make that commitment. It's fine if you don't want to; I get it. But you're not going to have the success you say you want if you're not willing to sacrifice.

Working with young people today also takes a different approach. I hired a millennial. Let's just say it didn't work out. When he left, he said that he was going to go find an easier job. That was his thing. He went to work in a call center at Comcast.

In this business you have to find somebody who is hungry, humble, and smart. It's not people smart, it's real-life smart. It's not book smart, it's real world. Can I understand people? Can I figure out what I need to be doing next? You have to have somebody who's quick thinking. I can have a conversation and I can tell you if you've got what it takes to make it out there.

If you're fumbling and you can't think of the next thing, if I throw a scenario at you, or if I'm talking to you and you don't have a comeback at some level, it's not going to work. This job requires you to be quick on your feet.

It's also important to note that you can't be a know-it-all. You have to be humble and curious. It's quick to figure out if somebody's all about them or all about the other situation. So yeah, they have to be able to quickly react. They have to be humble in the sense they can't be all about them. If they are, knock them out. It's not going to work.

They must be hungry enough to make it happen. I won't put anybody on a draw. I won't do it because, if they don't believe in themselves that they can get a deal in the door right away, then I don't want 'em.

Does the beginning of this story sound familiar?

Maybe it sounds like you, or someone else you may know. Either way, Nicole is still creating the ending to her story and anyone else in this industry can as well!

Josh's Story: An Interview with a Top Producer

Josh Mettle told me his story before, and when I started this book his story came to mind. I asked if I could interview him for this book, and share it. It is one of the most memorable stories I have heard. Its different from Nicole's story, where she was tired of what she was doing, Josh's success came out of necessity and survival. He was <u>forced</u> to start over from scratch in 2010 when he had only 4 loans in pipeline. Today, his team's yearly production will be around $285 Mill ($70m in his name personally and about $215m to other LOs on his team from the leads he has personally generated). There is so much we can all learn from his 17 years of experience in the industry.

Josh knows how to dream big, and he's had the drive and determination it takes to find success since day one, but it didn't happen without bumps in the road. His first day in the mortgage business was on September 11, 2001, believe it or not. Originally, his focus was on refinance and investor loan business and he had success in those business channels from the beginning. However, many of us know what happened to those channels in the late 2000's. Soon he had to start all over again and reinvent himself from scratch. Below are some of the transcripts from the interview I did with Josh. Sorry if the flow seems choppy. Josh is a great story teller and I had to omit parts of the interview for the sake of time. This is his story of how he went from 4 loans in his pipeline to becoming a Top Producer. He also gives a little insight into HOW he thinks and the Mindsets that got him where he is today.

Josh started his mortgage career in a call shop:

> *The job was to call a sheet of leads you were given, tell them that you're affiliated with the bank currently servicing their mortgage and try to get them to refinance their loan.*
>
> *You fill out a sheet, and then you turn that sheet in to your processor. From there your processor would enter the 1003 into the computer, pull credit, and basically tell you if you had a deal or not. But we were literally just a call center. I think I made around $70-$80,000 my first year, which wasn't bad for a 22-year-old kid.*

It took about 2 years before he crossed over to understanding loans and how to properly take loan applications. He then moved on to a larger brokerage and from there, a chorus line of banks.

"What sticks out to me in those early years, something my mom reminded me of, was I had this rule early on that I wouldn't go home until I had 10 of these applications (Mindset #5). It was all refinancing back then."

Within the first 2 years or so, Josh had already become systematic and proactive with his approach by making rules for himself, his first rule, "If I remember right, I'd make somewhere around 150 calls a day. About 1 out of every 15 calls you'd get a sheet filled out."

That was a self-imposed rule. Josh would dial until he got 10 applications or he actually woke 3 people up. "If I woke the third person up from calling them, that was my cutoff point-where, okay, quit being a menace to society and go home. Tomorrow's a new day."

Josh was regimented from day one. He was determined at an early age to have a certain level of success.

He grew up with a single mom and things were not easy for them:

> *We were in LA at the time where gunshots, screaming and sirens were not unusual at all. I mean, that was kind of like par for the course. I remember when I was 13 years*

> *old, we were shopping for groceries at the Food for Less grocery store. I'll never forget it as long as I live. The gal at the check-out register said, 'Assistance on aisle 9 for a food stamps purchase.' I was like, 'Who are they talking about? We're on aisle 9.' Then it hit me, I was like, 'Oh shit that's us. We're on food stamps!'*

He remembers his mom hocking her wedding ring for money for food.

"We never went without food. We always had a meal, but none of them were easy. Mom was kicking and fighting, and scratching and clawing to make sure we had 3 square meals a day." Josh made the decision at a young age, "… that would not be a problem for me and my family."

He knew early on that he was going to figure out how to make money and that was never going to be a problem for him in his life.

"So, if it took making calls till 9:00 at night or waking 3 people up, that was just a minor inconvenience compared to watching my mom hock her wedding ring for food."

Fast forwarding a few years right before the mortgage crisis hit, Josh was a correspondent mortgage banker and luckily, by that point, things had really started to turn around both for Josh and his mom:

> *My mom ended up going back to college and got her law degree at age 50. She was*

the oldest graduating law student ever at that university. She ended up going into private practice where she started representing landlords who were evicting tenants that weren't paying their rent.

Those same landlords who were her clients were having a difficult time getting mortgage financing and finding a mortgage banker that could understand a little bit more of a complex, affluent borrower, get theirs loans out quickly and on time, and do what they said they would do. I became the lender they could count on.

Josh ramped up in the investment world. Not only was he personally buying investment properties, but he was doing a lot of loans for investors:

In fact, I was just talking to a guy yesterday from Countrywide that worked under Anthony Mozilo under the fast and easy days. He remembered me because our branch in Salt Lake City had the #1 loan officer in the country for Countrywide for a quarter. That was me in 2006 or 2007.

That business primarily came from clients buying investment properties:

It was the first year that I ever cracked seven figures, and it was just me and an assistant. We were cranking out 25 to 40

> *loans a month. All purchase business by this time, most of them investors. Of course, it was fast and easy back then. At 29 or 30 years old, we had gone from hocking wedding rings to making seven figures, things looked great.*

Just when things were going great for Josh, the bottom fell out. "My investor friends and builder friends got obliterated, just wiped off the face of the earth." Josh remembers a particular bottom moment he had while at a mortgage conference in Las Vegas. "It was in early- or mid-December, which is a weird time for a conference. I was clearing out that month's pipeline, updating what we had closed, and looking at the pipeline for January. I think that was January 2009. I had 4 loans in the pipeline." As he scanned ahead, he realized he didn't have any loans for February.

"I went back and looked at January of the previous year, and I had closed 32 loans." He went from 32 loans in January of the past year to having 4 loans total in the pipeline to start the next year. "Unfortunately, my spending had not curtailed. ... I had a new Rover in the garage, a new Mercedes in the garage, a new house that I was living in. I was also under contract to move into another house."

If something didn't drastically change within the next 60 days, Josh was at an extreme risk of bankruptcy. "I had no savings at all. I just had properties that you couldn't sell right now in this market and 4 loans in the pipeline." Being out of town at a conference and coming to this realization is terrible timing but it turned into a blessing.

There was a guy at the conference, "... a younger guy, probably 30-ish, 35-ish, so right around my age, at the time. I believe he was living in California." The crash in California had hit a year or 2 before it really hit Utah, where Josh is from. "We thought we were going to escape it because, you know, we are in Utah!"

Josh explained the young man at the conference from California had gotten a team of realtors and contractors together and they were going in and buying distressed properties for pennies on the dollar. The contractors would fix them, his realtor partner would sell them, and he would do the financing. That guy orchestrated the whole thing, and his business went from 3 loans a month to him and his team doing 40 loans a month.

The realization was that not everybody was failing. Someone had figured out the right Mindset. "In the middle of this crash, this guy's going to make a couple million bucks a year. If he can figure it out, why not me?"

After doing his pipeline review, he said he almost didn't go back into the conference. "I almost decided to like, go gamble or start drinking, but something got me back into that conference and I watched that kid's presentation." That presentation turned into the decision to hire his first coach. "That was probably one of the most pivotal, direction changing moments in my life." Josh decided to hire the same coach that was interviewing the kid on stage. "I showed him an $8,000 check that I did not have, and by the grace of God, I escaped the crash and barely made it out."

The first thing he did when he got home was create a future vision since he couldn't use his past experience to guide him. The coach had Josh create a life plan and a business plan for what Josh wanted things to look like in the future. He gave Josh hope that, "even though things were falling apart, if we create and implement a plan, we could successfully navigate [through this recession] and survive."

My coach said, "You know, the cool thing is, when you start over from scratch, you get to rebuild it the way you want it."

"Sometimes you chase success and end up going down a path that maybe you didn't want to go down. That was really impactful to me; 1 to have a plan and 2, to think about how I want to build it so that it works for me (Mindset #5)."

That was the springboard which started Josh thinking down the lines of consumer direct marketing. "That was just a starting place, and it evolved over years to come."

The first thing Josh did after creating the life plan and the business plan was to start filming videos to send to past clients talking to them about refinancing:

> *We started leveraging technology. We started using video. I had gotten out of the refinance business because I'd done all those investor loans.*

During the first couple of those "reinventing" years, Josh was pretty hungry. "I was there 8:00 in the morning working with my processor. I would leave in the afternoon to go to the gym and I'd come back and dial until probably about 8:00- 9:00 at night." This cycle would repeat each day.

Obviously, the crash made Josh change how he thought, and it changed who he was. Coaching helped him figure out there's a different path, but mentally, what was it that gave Josh the confidence to go down that path? I asked him in the interview.

"I think it goes back to that initial decision as a kid that it really didn't matter what it was going to take. I wasn't going to worry about money." Josh remembers thinking:

> *Would I kill for money? Would I steal for money? It was a real commitment regardless of what I'm going to have to do (Mindset #1). Thankfully, I had some good people in my life and I didn't have to go*

> *down those roads. I remembered, when I came back from that event, my schedule started to change.*

Josh explained he had always been a morning guy because he was getting his workouts in the morning. "I'd go to bed about 8:00, and I would sleep about 4.5–5 hours. And I did that for a couple of years."

Josh was studying marketing and reinventing his strategies daily. "I would wake up at like 1:30. I'd drink my coffee while I was reviewing my life plan. I'd study direct marketing for a couple hours and then my wife and I would go to the gym by 6:00AM. Little bit of email in there." That schedule, even with only 4 loans, started with the decision that he was not going to be financially strapped. "I certainly was not going to bring a child into this world and be financially strapped."

If that required only getting 4 hours of sleep, so be it. That wasn't a big deal for Josh.

He did this for 3 or 4 years, devoting 3 hours of his morning to studying direct response marketing:

> *I mean, I was doing online webinars, I was paying for courses, I was reading their newsletters, I was reading their books. I was literally digesting content for 3 hours a day, 5 days a week in the morning (Mindset #8).*

> *I was reading non-industry stuff and figuring out how to apply it to my industry, nothing mortgage related whatsoever (Mindset #1). The mortgage industry was still talking about short sales, the sky is falling, Bank of America is under, and now Washington Federal is under, etc.*

Josh was reading guys like Frank Kern and Eben Pagan. Eben Pagan made $10 million in one year marketing dating advice online. Ten million dollars in one year was unheard-of during this period. "Well, here's this group of people in real estate, figuring out how to short sale and declare bankruptcies to stay in their house as long as possible without getting evicted over here, but then there are these guys over here making $10 million in their underwear from online marketing."

Since those guys seemed to be having a lot more fun. Josh decided to go study what they're doing.

While taking their webinars and reading their books he realized it's like speaking a different language. It took about six months to learn the language, and then Josh started to really see the similarities and figured out how to implement what he learned in his own marketing.

That jived with his beliefs about rebuilding on your own terms:

> *I hate chasing realtors, it just drives me nuts. I can't stand begging for business. I*

try to drive value, but even now, I struggle with the whole concept of realtor sales meetings, and this, that, and the other. It just goes against who I am just a little bit. I'm getting better at it, but I struggle with it.

I prefer going directly to the consumer by figuring out what's their problem, who's underserved, and with that, creating a solution to get to them in a media format that makes them respond asking for additional information. That's direct response marketing.

Within a year, Josh went from 3 hours of studying in the morning to an hour of studying in the morning. The other 2 or 3 hours he had to work with in the morning were devoted to working on loans.

By the end of that year, Josh had started to see results. "I got myself back into that 10–12 loans a month range by the end of that very first year. Then it just kind of grew from there."

To go from 4 loans (that were all investment loans) to 10-12 loans, Josh had to completely reinvent and start over:

I literally didn't have one client left. I did not have one realtor left at that point. Today, I'm re-working with one of those initial clients, but besides that, every realtor, every investor client I had

> *completely got wiped out. And I don't think I've done a loan for any of them since then.*

Josh was extremely strategic on what he was doing. He studied a lot and was implementing fast. It was all trial and error. Josh told me about seminars of Dan Kennedy's that he would fly to:

> *There would be a mega seminar where a thousand people would come from every industry, from plumbers to aero-science, every different, diverse business owner and entrepreneur. They'd come and talk about what they're using in their businesses. Dan wrote newsletters every month that would talk about the same things, highlighting specific people who had implemented his theories and his advice, and then show how they were using it in their industry.*
>
> *I would take that little piece the plumber was doing, or dry cleaner was doing, and I would try to figure out how that was relatable to mortgages. Then, I'd write a newsletter and send that out to my past clients... I'd film a video and send it out to my past clients. I would just try and roll it into whatever I could find that was relatable.*
>
> *Every month, when the newsletter would come I'd highlight all the pitches and ideas. I'd pick 1 or 2, and we would implement that idea the next month into our marketing.*

That was about the time that Josh hired his first marketing person.

He had a great plan for a team (Mindset #4). "By that time I had a loan officer assistant, and then a marketing person. That marketing person really took on the implementation. Bless them!"

In a recent podcast with Dan Sullivan at Strategic Coach and Peter Diamandis from the X Prize, they discussed this concept of "who, not what".

In other words, when you come up with an idea as an entrepreneur, your first thought process should not be, "What do I need to do?"

It should be:

"Who do I need to hire or bring alongside me to accomplish this goal?"

When it comes to implementation, Josh was doing that. Not to the level they're describing, but he was taking baby steps towards the "who, not what", when it came to implementation.

By this time, he had a one-year-old baby and was still doing workouts in the morning with his wife. He was still studying, creating the content for his marketing, doing loans, and building a team. He had to find the "who" that could really implement and pull these things off:

> *I mean, if you're going to create your own mailing and mail out to 500 people, that's a lot of freaking work.*

> *Before you find a "who", you have to work 20 hours a day to get the wheels moving to get enough revenue coming in and prove your model, so you can hire the "who".*
>
> *People sometimes forget that. People think, 'Oh, I'm doing five loans a month and all it's going to take me to get to 10 is to hire somebody. Well that may be true for some rare cases, but you must be economically viable on your own. Your business model must be dialed in and systems already in place (Mindsets #2 & #4). Improve your own model before you hire that person to get you to 15. It took a year, maybe a year and a half of doing everything until I got enough money rolling in so I could then go to the owner of the company at that time and say, 'Hey, I'm doing 10 or 12 loans a month, but I think I can get to 15 or 20. Will you help pay for a marketing person?' That was my "who" to step up the implementation a notch."*
>
> *That's a different conversation with your boss than, 'Hey, I'm only closing 4 loans a month; I need you guys to do something to help me?'*

Josh believes that's not advisable:

> *If I'm only closing 4 loans a month, that's on me. You have to burn the midnight oil and get a little more hustle (Mindset #3). When you get to 10, 12, or 15 loans a*

> *month, you need some help. You probably need some mentorship or leadership as to who that hire should be. I didn't really have that mentorship or leadership. I just figured it out. It'd sure be nice to go up to someone in your world and say, 'Man, I'm at 10, 11, 12, I want to go to 20. What's my next move?'*
>
> *If you're only doing 4 a month, that's on you, not on anybody else. That's not a ceiling. That's a work ethic problem.*

At this stage in his career, Josh is also driven by competition. "The first person I compete with is me getting old." Josh turned 40 in June and had a goal to be in the best shape of his life at 40. "I'm definitely in better shape now than when I was 18. Hands down. It's silly to compete with myself, but I try to make things hard on myself (Mindset #7)."

He gave another example of this:

> *I have a stand-up desk, I try and stand for eight to ten hours and not sit except for, my doctor friend told me I must sit when I eat. If I'm eating at my desk, I must sit for that. But besides that, I try to stand, and that kind of sucks. But I do it just because it's hard, and it's a way for me to compete with myself and keep my edge a little bit because my life's gotten pretty comfortable.*

I also compete with my wife. She's younger than me and in better shape. We go to fitness classes together and I compete against her workout as well as try to improve against my previous workouts. I compete with myself that way too.

We talk a lot in our branch about time integrity. We have time throughout the day when the whole branch is scheduled for prospecting time. I try to compete with myself to get a perfect day on time integrity, where all I'm doing is prospecting. It's incredibly hard (Mindset #5). As you know, you got recruits, you got your own loans, and you got 20 other loan officers' loans. It's incredibly hard to ask for 2 hours of time integrity where you're doing nothing but that one task.

And then I'm definitely competing with the 26 companies that are currently above us in our market. Our CEO said, 'We should be number one or number 2 in the market, or we should get out.' So, I thought, well, that sounds like a damn fun game. I'm in. Sign me up for that one.

Josh's company started tracking the rankings of who's above them in terms of production:

When we first got the rankings, we were 58th or 56th in our market. Would you like being 56th on any list? Nobody would. That pissed me off. This year, we've moved

> *from 56th to 27th. My current competition, I would say, or my current game right now involves my daughter that leaves for college in 12 years. She's my youngest. And by the time she leaves for college, I want to be number 1 or number 2, jockeying for that top couple positions.*
>
> *By that time, I'll be 52, and that begins the unwinding phase a little bit. I'm not saying I want to retire at 52, I just want to start giving big pieces of the pie to other people who helped me get there, and to start taking on less and start hanging out with my wife a little bit more. A lot more.*

I wanted to hear more about Josh's time management. Josh revealed he keeps his schedule in Outlook. His daily routine, or algorithm, or schedule is in Outlook forever:

> *I'm sure you've heard this analogy before. You have a fish bowl, or a fish tank, a five-pound bag of sand, and five pounds of rocks. How do you get it all in?*

(Ok I did not prompt him on this example. Ironic I know. And yes, I had already written in that analogy in 5th Mindset before we did this interview).

> *Put the rocks in first, and then you pour the sand around the rocks. If you put the sand in first, the rocks will stick out the top of the fish bowl.*

For me, it's meditation and no technology upon rising. It's coffee. I have to have coffee. Water, coffee, vitamins, meditation. Then it's a quick review of the life and business plan, which is linked together in an appointment in my Outlook calendar. Then it's on to a big project I'm working on for an hour. I get about 30 minutes to clean up email. Then it's the gym, breakfast with the family, and then I am in the office by 8:15 for a gratitude meeting, then prospecting from 8:30–10:30. Those are the rocks. Those do not move.

Those things might change if you're on vacation or something like that, but when you get back, that is the foundation. I have those weekly meetings that are set. Then from there, everything else fills in. It's like the sand around the rocks. I have to be out of the office at 5:30. I personally put myself responsible for picking up kids and doing stuff like that. It starts at 5:30.

My schedule has the rocks, from the routine in the morning to the people that I need to meet with weekly or quarterly. Everything else fills in as the sand around the rocks. My team knows they can fill in my schedule around those, with appointments with clients, realtors, etc. They have free access to do that.

One of Josh's rocks, on the business side, includes prospecting for 2 hours. Prospecting is kind of a broad term that everybody uses. During that time, what is the prospecting Josh is doing? Who is it?

> *Our CRM has all our leads, realtors, past clients, and under-contracts in it and the system gives us automated cues, which are tasks, to follow up with those leads, under-contracts, past clients, and realtors. The 2 hours spent prospecting should be spent in your outbox and not looking at inbound emails. It's incredibly difficult to be disciplined to do that. You are in your CRM dialing leads, trying to get them to move to the next step. It should be spent having phone conversations, reviewing past clients' loans, doing loan reviews, and calling your best realtors. It's outbound communication via phone, text, email, and video that you would not have had otherwise if you hadn't put that time in your schedule. You would've gotten side tracked responding to the emergency of the moment or Facebook for 15 minutes or whatever.*
>
> *Prospecting is a disciplined time of outbound communication to as many past clients, current, clients, prospects, realtors, etc. It's where you're reaching outwardly to people that are potentially in the business of needing a mortgage.*

If somebody has done 4 loans a month for the last 4 years but knows there's something more, Josh has more advice on what they should change:

> *There's this great Jim Carrey quote that says, and I'm going to butcher it, but basically says, 'Oftentimes, people disguise fear as practicality.' The first thing I want to know from that person doing 4 loans a month is, 'What are you afraid of? What's holding you back? What in your mind is not allowing you to throttle forward?'*
>
> *My guess is they'd give you some response that sounds like, 'It's not practical with my work environment or my home environment,' or, 'It's not practical with all my responsibilities,' or maybe, 'I don't like to work that much.' That's not really how humans are built. Humans are built and where they're happiest, when they are challenged, and they're improving.*
>
> *I would ask them, 'Why are you doing 4 or 5 loans a month?' If they gave me some reason based in practicality, I would try and figure out if there is really some fear there. I'll give you an example. If someone says, 'I don't want to do more loans because I don't want to take time away from my family.' Totally, I get it, but if you do 1 more loan or 2 more loans, you can hire an assistant. And then you get a bunch*

more time with your family. Then, by the way, when you go home, instead of mowing your lawn for 2 hours, you can hire somebody to do that too, so you have time to take your kid fishing on Saturday. Where is that fear that's keeping them there? That'd be my first thing.

Let's build a plan. Where do you want to go? Give me a future vision. How do we want to get there? Make a plan and just start executing that plan as fast as possible. That's different for everybody.

Maybe you are someone who can walk into a room full of realtors, and by the time you walk out, you have a room full of friends. Maybe you have a gift with that. That's not my gift. I would have someone identify where their personal strengths are, and then have them create a schedule and a routine that allows them to shine energy on that personal strength.

If you're a people person, you need to figure out where the realtors are. You need to be out of the office, looking for groups of people to meet with. This should be a priority and something that's in your schedule. You need to be the mayor of mortgage.

Josh believes you should start by identifying your strengths. Then build a plan that focuses on utilizing that strength every day, day after day.

This becomes a rock in your schedule that you do without thought or hesitation.

I asked Josh what he thinks are the 3 most important things that make a good loan officer great:

> *Having a vision, being committed, and confidence. You must get your mind right first.*
>
> *Confidence is important because if you can't believe in yourself, how are you going to sell yourself to anybody else?*
>
> *I was meeting with a friend of mine, Charlotte (Mindset #8). She's the top loan officer for a competitor and she's been a $100 million producer for the past 15-20 years. She told me she had to remind herself of the value she brought to each client because her company didn't have the best rates.*
>
> *She said, 'I have to remind myself that my clients get Charlotte, it's going to be a fantastic experience and I will get them to the closing table.'*
>
> *You need to have confidence in what you bring to the table as a loan officer and how you can serve clients. You want to have confidence to the point where, if someone shuts you down or rejects you, you can say, 'Your loss. Next.' You want the next person you get on the phone with to feel your*

> *confidence so that the logical decision is to choose you.*

Let's look at Josh's story again. What do you think the average LO would have done in these situations Josh faced? Here are a few observations:

- For starters, the average LO wouldn't have even been at that event where he heard that young guy speaking!

- If they were, they probably would have been gambling or in the bar.

- With a huge drop in their pipeline, the average LO probably wouldn't spend the money to ask for coaching help.

- They probably wouldn't have made the time or energy commitment to get up so early to study, explore, or reinvent themselves in the marketplace.

- The average LO wouldn't have taken it upon themselves to apply new ideas to our industry.

- The average LO probably would have blamed his boss or his company for everything they aren't doing ("Our rates are too high" or "you should get me an assistant").

- The average LO during that time sat and waited for the "market" to turn around.

> Josh hustled during that time and secured huge market share.

The average LO would have quit. As many did during that time.

Conclusion?

It's not true that top producing Loan Originators are all great sales people, marketing geniuses, guideline experts, database geeks, networking gurus, perfect relationship managers, AND well-connected social butterflies.

What makes them a great producer is HOW THEY THINK and WHERE THEY FOCUS THEIR EFFORTS! That's what separates them from the pack. It's all in their Mindset(s).

Many of the Top 1% Loan Originators share the same 8 Mindsets. The good news is wherever you are as a Loan Originator; you have the ability to evolve your thinking. Changing a few concepts can make a HUGE impact for yourself, your family, your employees, and your customers.

What steps should a LO, who wants to grow their business, take? As you have seen there are many paths a LO could choose. Here are a few suggestions from Top LO's:

1. Develop a passion for the industry. We are changing lives daily. Don't look at it as "just a job."
2. That passion will develop your competitive spirit. Your volume (and pocketbook) will be your scorecard.
3. Take the time to write it out. What's the vision of your business in the future? This should be built around your unique abilities and your strengths. As you read from Nicole and Josh's stories, their visions are completely different and yours will be too. We all have different strengths.
4. Get a coach. There are many good ones out there. They can see things in you that you can't see yourself.
5. Put the work in. You may need to work crazy hours initially. Do it. Its only temporary until you have the momentum for self-sustainment. It's a small price to pay for a great future for you and your family.
6. Implement new ideas FAST
7. Constantly evaluate where you are and where you need to improve. Every season brings new issues and opportunities. Be thankful for where you are, but never stop trying to improve. You can use our scorecard to help evaluate where you are.

"The journey of a thousand miles begins with a single step."
-Lao Tzu

Want to see how your scorecard measures up to Nicole's and Josh's? After completing your own scorecard, email me at: team@loignite.com and I will be happy to forward them.

The LO Scorecard discussed in this book not only helps you uncover how you currently "measure up," but will also give you a roadmap to become a Top Producer.

> **Step 1:** Go to **lopotential.com** to fill out your own Loan Officer Mindset Scorecard and see how you match up to the 1%ers.
>
> **Step 2:** Keep working and improving your scorecard score and see what a big difference a small change in thinking makes.
>
> **Step 3:** Each quarter retake the scorecard and don't stop till you reach the top.

Most loan officers work too hard reacting to all the situations they find themselves in; that prevents them from getting out there and creating the life they know they can have.

Now with the Mindsets the top producers embrace you can take your business to whatever level you want it to be.

If you'd like our help, go to **lopotential.com** and get started.

Your Top Loan Officer Potential Scorecard

Here's how to get the most from your Top Loan Officer Potential Scorecard.

While looking at each Mindset, see which of the four stages resonates with you most. Within that stage, there are then three scores to choose from.

A lower score would indicate an opportunity to reinforce that stage, a higher score indicates an opportunity to transition to the next level.

Is there a weakness? Are you solidly entrenched in this stage? Or are you on the verge of moving to the next level?

The assessment offers a qualitative view, especially in stage four and the differential points between 10 and 12.

If you are at point 12, you are completely focused and "in the zone" within that Mindset, whereas if you are at point 10, there is plenty of room for improvement.

Remember, none of the top producers we interviewed gave themselves a 12 in any area. They all felt there was room for improvement.

By grading yourself on a quarterly basis, you can see where you can make improvements. You can assess your position, and then set objectives and focus for the quarter ahead.

Mindset One: Personal Growth & Ambition

Description	Score
You are frightened by changes and prefer things to stay as they currently are. You are not interested in change or growth.	1 2 3
You are starting to understand the possibilities of growth in all areas of your life, though you feel stuck.	4 5 6
You've experienced an acceptable status level and wish to maintain this level. You're not interested in further growth requiring more effort.	7 8 9
You always look for ways to grow and people who can help you become a better version of yourself. You may have a Business/Life Coach.	10 11 12
Score:	
Goal:	

Mindset Two: CEO Mindset

You feel your company should provide direction for your business future & you depend on their support to determine your success.	1 2 3
You understand the concepts of being self-made and try to align with a company that will help support your desired growth.	4 5 6
You work to improve your skills, but feel your company/manager should be responsible to provide the tools needed to succeed.	7 8 9
You treat your business like "You, Inc." You have marketing/business plans & you do not rely on others to invest in your success.	10 11 12
Score:	
Goal:	

Mindset Three: Sense of Urgency

You are afraid of doing things that others may perceive as "pushy" & you tend to let life happen at its own pace & aren't quick to act.	1
	2
	3
You are beginning to realize that you need to act quickly to seize opportunities in your life, yet you don't know how to do it.	4
	5
	6
You find there are times when you have acted quickly & it has helped you and others, yet you find it hard to do when the stakes are highest.	7
	8
	9
Your belief is that things need to happen right now before something changes and you relentlessly encourage others to move now.	10
	11
	12
Score:	
Goal:	

Mindset Four: Your Team

You do not see the benefit in adding a member to your team, or you would not want the responsibility.	1 2 3
You feel an assistant or partner could be helpful, but you haven't figured out how to fund them or how they would fit into your system.	4 5 6
You have at least 1 other member on your team and you have clearly defined roles for each person.	7 8 9
You have a full production team that predictably generates business whether you are in the office or not. Each member knows their role.	10 11 12
Score:	
Goal:	

Mindset Five: Systematic & Proactive	
You start each day without a plan. You are best at winging it.	1 2 3
Most of your day is spent reacting to phone calls and emails. Your best intentions sometimes take the back seat to the crisis of the moment.	4 5 6
You have created systems that limit crisis management, giving you more time to prospect for new business.	7 8 9
You map out your days which keeps you focused on business generating activities regardless of what's going on around you.	10 11 12
Score:	
Goal:	

Mindset Six: Production Results

Your average 12 Month Productions is: Less than 5 loans per month.	1
	2
	3
Your average 12 Month Productions is: 6-10 loans per month.	4
	5
	6
Your average 12 Month Productions is: 10-20 loans per month.	7
	8
	9
Your average 12 Month Productions is: 21+ loans per month.	10
	11
	12
Score:	
Goal:	

Mindset Seven: Competitive Mindset

Statement	Score
You feel competition is only for athletes and do not care about how you rank amongst your peers.	1 / 2 / 3
You want to win personally & professionally in all areas of your life but aren't sure how to succeed.	4 / 5 / 6
You like to win at the things you deem important and feel the effort is more important than the results.	7 / 8 / 9
You want to win at everything you do, and you are willing to put forth whatever effort is needed to guarantee victory.	10 / 11 / 12
Score:	
Goal:	

Mindset Eight: Industry Lifestyle	
You feel you should always separate business & pleasure, and treat each closing as a business transaction.	**1**
	2
	3
You'd like to find others with your same Mindset to collaborate with but aren't sure where to find these groups to reach out.	4
	5
	6
You go to industry events and enjoy socializing at these events but prefer not talking shop during your personal time.	7
	8
	9
You enjoy talking shop with friends, family & clients. You don't consider it "work". Hanging out with others in "Biz" is fun, like a hobby.	**10**
	11
	12
Score:	
Goal:	

Your Loan Officer Potential Scorecard

	Score	Goal
Growth and Ambition		
CEO Mindset		
Sense of Urgency		
Your Team		
Systematic and Proactive		
Productive		
Competitive Mindset		
Industry Lifestyle		

Score:	
Goal:	
Date:	
Mood:	

Made in the USA
Coppell, TX
18 November 2019